Aquarians with Summer Babies

Jennifer Hilder

Presentation by *BookLeaf Publishing*

Web: www.bookleafpub.com

E-mail: info@bookleafpub.com

ISBN: 9789357615914

First edition 2022

The coffee shop

The old man sits on a worn brown leather stool
Coffee cup in hand, slight tremor
Watching the busy workers
The one with black hair and even blacker eyes
talks and talks
The pastries glow eerily under the false light
Waiting for napkins to take them away
Lonely sugar longing for a hungry soul
The woman with the yellow hair leans against
the counter,
listening, waiting for her turn to talk
Drooping shoulders,
Twisted napkins, used and discarded
Sticky fingers.
The cold outside waits, patiently.

Devoured,
Hungry,
Waiting,
Twisted

unconscious

lovely awakening
brings me here
to consciousness
my dreams dissipate
lightly floating through the air
as I grasp desperately
with my mind
trying to hold onto
the fleeting images
and important messages
messages from myself
for me to unravel
the harder I try
the further they float
until I can no
longer see them
if I could
listen in the present
moment
I would be so wise
the doorways that
don't exist
they turn into
crawlspaces in closets
or simply into walls

Stranger

I am afraid of who will be looking back at me…
with those eyes in the mirror
I used to fear the stranger there,
the one with my face.
Ideas brought on by
Scary stories
Fascination with horror
It was so far away
Until it was closer
When it walked into my home
And looked at me with eyes that don't belong
Now I fear the
Stranger there, waiting
Ready to surprise me
Only now, the eyes are mine
Looking back at me
Trapped in unfamiliar surroundings,
Someone else's face
The deepest part
An everchanging ocean
If I look in them too long
Where do I go?

Night

My face does not
even show in
the background

bright
lively

It shows through
the window
the darkness
hiding in
the corner

I wait 'till
they see me
then I
wake up

For you

I go for a wander suddenly
Turning with you
Like dark rain
Deep Blue empty fling

These waves vanish
As you throw drops of storm about us
I lie open and wait

For you

See Me

Your eyes do not always
    see me
    and sometimes
    don't
    even turn my way.

Our lips lock through
our eyes, smiling open
That feeling of knowing,
that feeling of pain
that feeling of shame

trees

Out there
waiting
looking
time flying by
a hawk
riding the wind
The trees stand there
every day
I look at them
I shudder for their nakedness to the world
their stubborn stance
unwilling and unable
to run away

I am

I am afraid
of the dark
I am afraid of
the way you look at me

I cannot fool myself
as I sit here and contemplate
something
that has already been decided
before I even
entered the room.
Her rhythmic voice
brings me here
and I lean in to hear the magic
I listen
but they don't make sense.
The ground has stopped shaking.
I have made up my mind.
I am strong
I am.

Wallpaper

There is a house with slaughterhouse wallpaper
There is a man and a woman and a fridge full of
meat
They looked at each other and saw their own
loneliness
Their own despair
We are living graves
She said with a smile
He looked at her with pasty eyes
Displacing the blame but looking befuddled
They slaved in their lives
They ate tragedy and anguish
Then they ate each other's tears
The blood left stains on their souls

Sea

The waves circle the seaweed
A boat rocks
While a seagull rests on a cliff

One crab left,
Four dolphins
And a million plates of feathers and fins

Gone

So many words, left unsaid
I wanted to say them while looking in your eyes
So I waited
Now you are gone.
Who am I supposed to say these unsaid words to
now?
Whose eyes are gonna tell me the truth?

times with the other oNe

The first time shouldn't have happened,
not like that
I wanted it too much
there was this power imbalance
there was cat shit on the bed
Should have taken that as a sign
Not just moved it out of the way

Outside

As she watches the rocks skip past her
She hurls one down below in anger and betrayal
of herself
And things fall out of her mouth to the ground
Falling on deaf ears and particles of nothingness
Bugs flying, lighting the way for the weary
woman of her soul
All alone, and so outcast, she almost cried
But for the tears unshed, lying upon her floor
Waiting to be let up onto the bed and into their
hearts
Of total despair and tragic love
An unforgiving ending

the other oNe

He held my hand as if it were normal
The feeling of his hand and my hand brought too
much joy and I almost pulled away
But I didn't
Instead, I looked into his eyes trying to figure
him out
His eyes laughed at me kindly, as they always
did
I kept my hand in his as they talked about their
new baby
Isn't that a beautiful name he asked me?
I said it was and I was being honest, it was true,
it was beautiful

Other Past Ghosts

Those days gone
along with other past ghosts
the lingering anger
well below the surface
so long
threatening to get out

New stillness
more uncertainty

Other lifetimes

Isolated daisies
in a still Italian pond
my tears
you rid
a loss
so old
and so
long
ago

My Fathers Father

A room full of nightmares
the window with the white curtain shakes and
shatters
GIANT boulders .... and even bigger feelings of
dread
hanging in the air by a thread
and below, everything buried.

The pain of you

The pain of losing you the first time has made it
difficult to trust you this time
Yet, I do anyways
My heart a delicate mush in your virtual hands
You think it is just sexual
I think it is the stars aligning in total symmetry,
boundless beauty that only fades in the light of
your masculine energy
Fading away with the other shriveled flowers,
pushed aside in the name of passion